Original title:
Embracing the Journey

Copyright © 2024 Swan Charm
All rights reserved.

Author: Sebastian Sarapuu
ISBN HARDBACK: 978-9916-89-619-8
ISBN PAPERBACK: 978-9916-89-620-4
ISBN EBOOK: 978-9916-89-621-1

Why We Wander

In search of dreams, we roam far,
Beneath the bright, guiding star.
With every step, the heart will sigh,
For the unknown calls us to try.

The whispers of the wind do tease,
Through tangled woods and swaying trees.
A compass spins, yet time won't bind,
Adventures waiting, tales unwind.

Mountains rise, water flows strong,
Nature hums her ancient song.
Through valleys deep and skies so wide,
We seek the truth that cannot hide.

With gentle grace, the paths will weave,
A dance of fate, we dare believe.
In every turn, a lesson learned,
The flame of curiosity burned.

So take my hand, let's lose our way,
In this great world, come what may.
Together we'll chase the setting sun,
For wandering souls are never done.

The Tapestry of Wanderlust

Threads of dreams intertwine and bend,
As we journey, there's no end.
Colors blend, where hearts ignite,
In the tapestry of day and night.

Footprints left on sandy shores,
Echoes whisper, open doors.
Every place, a story told,
In wanderlust, we become bold.

Mountains stand with tales to share,
Clouds drift softly in warm air.
The sky's a canvas, wild and free,
Painted hues of destiny.

With each sunrise, a new delight,
Chasing stars in the velvet night.
Embrace the path, both rough and smooth,
In the dance of life, we find our groove.

So let our spirits roam and play,
In the tapestry, we find our way.
For with each journey, near or far,
We become the dreams that we are.

Footfalls of the Brave

With every footfall, courage grows,
In shadows thick, the true light glows.
Hearts bold enough to face the fight,
Forge ahead into the night.

Across the fields of green and gold,
Stories waiting to be told.
Each step whispers a sacred vow,
To seek the unknown, here and now.

The mountains stand, they sway and bend,
Guardians strong, they will defend.
Through storms and trials, we must strive,
For it's the brave who will survive.

With the wind as our faithful guide,
We embrace the wild, with arms open wide.
In the echoes of our laughter's sound,
The footprints of the brave are found.

So gather courage, let it lead,
In every heart, there's a seed.
For those who wander, strive, and dare,
Make footprints in the open air.

The Rhythm of Every Footstep

In the quiet of the night,
Soft whispers of the street,
Each step a fleeting beat,
Guiding hearts to take flight.

Shadows dance beneath the moon,
Echoes of stories untold,
As time moves swiftly, bold,
A melody ending too soon.

The pulse of the ground we tread,
A symphony of our pace,
With hopes we quietly trace,
Every tune in our head.

Through alleys dark, paths unknown,
With each stride, a new refrain,
We carry joy, loss, and pain,
A journey we call our own.

In the rhythm of our way,
We find strength, love, and grace,
Every footfall leaves a trace,
Life's dance unfolds in sway.

Dreams Bloom in Unpredictable Soil

In gardens where seeds are sown,
Hope springs forth in strange places,
Worn hands trace the dream's faces,
Unseen roots, softly grown.

The winds whisper tales anew,
As petals burst to the light,
In darkness, they find their fight,
Colors bleed, vibrant and true.

Every storm that comes our way,
Nurtures dreams with wild grace,
In chaos, we find a space,
For blossoms to start their play.

From the cracks of barren land,
Emerging blooms defy the odds,
Hope blooms fierce, against all gods,
Life's beauty, forever grand.

In the dance of chance, we thrive,
Embracing what nature brings,
From unexpected beginnings,
We learn finally to strive.

Capturing Moments on the Fly

A flash of light, a heartbeat,
Life unfolds in fleeting scenes,
Memories drift like soft dreams,
Caught within time's quick fleet.

With laughter ringing around,
We freeze the seconds in frames,
Life's essence, wild and untamed,
In a world spinning sound.

In glances shared, warmth ignites,
Moments caught in the stillness,
In the rush, we find the fullness,
A snapshot of pure delights.

With every click, we treasure,
Fragments of laughter and tears,
All the hopes, all the fears,
We hold close in pure pleasure.

Life moves fast, yet we recall,
The beauty of each captured view,
Snapshots of me and of you,
In these moments, we stand tall.

The Mystique of Every Bend

Around the corner, what awaits?
A story wrapped in silence,
In shadows, hidden brilliance,
The thrill of life abates.

As twisting paths wind along,
Curves hold secrets we chase,
Discoveries in every place,
An unsung, whispered song.

With each turn, new tales arise,
Enigmas softly unfold,
Like treasures made of pure gold,
Fueling our curious eyes.

The road beckons, calling near,
"To wander, embrace the unknown,"
In each bend, we've truly grown,
Facing our doubts, shedding fear.

In the labyrinth of life's trail,
Every corner, a fresh start,
An adventure in our hearts,
Where wonder will always prevail.

With Every Mile Comes a Story

On the road, where dreams collide,
Whispers of the past abide.
Each turn reveals a brand new scene,
Where hope and heartache weave between.

Mountains high and valleys low,
In every shadow, memories grow.
The laughter shared, the tears we shed,
In every mile, a tale is fed.

A child's giggle, an elder's sigh,
A fleeting moment, time rushing by.
The sun sets golden, the moon takes flight,
Stories linger long into the night.

With every stranger that we greet,
A bond is forged, a chance to meet.
In every journey, lessons learned,
Through every twist, our passions burned.

As horizons beckon, we find our way,
Through paths unseen, both night and day.
With every mile, horizons expand,
In every step, the world at hand.

The Dance Between Here and There

In twilight's glow, the world can sway,
Between the now and yesterday.
Each step a pulse, each breath a beat,
The dance of life beneath our feet.

Here stands still, with memories dear,
While there awaits with dreams unclear.
The pull of both, a sweet romance,
In every choice, we take a chance.

Footprints left on shifting sand,
Time slips by like grains in hand.
Amidst the doubt, the joy we find,
A tethered heart, but free in mind.

With every rhythm, a story spun,
The laughter shared, the battles won.
Each movement forward, a step in grace,
While shadows linger, we find our place.

So sway between the past and now,
Embrace the dance, take humble bow.
For in each moment, we learn to sing,
The beauty of the wandering.

The Joy of the Unexpected Detour

Beneath blue skies, plans often sway,
What starts as sure may drift away.
Yet in the bends, where paths diverge,
Adventure calls, and spirits surge.

Through winding roads and twists unknown,
Uncharted lands feel like homegrown.
The serendipity of the ride,
Where chance encounters gently guide.

Moments arise, unpredictable delight,
Under starlit skies and soft moonlight.
In what we find, we come alive,
In the unknown, our dreams arrive.

With laughter echoing through the breeze,
And whispered tales among the trees.
Every detour brings a bright surprise,
A hidden gem beneath the skies.

So let go of the straight and narrow,
Follow the bends, become the arrow.
In every twist, new joys in store,
The heart expands, forever wanting more.

Fragments of a Traveler's Soliloquy

Worn shoes tread on cobbled street,
Each echo holds the tales they greet.
In whispered winds, the stories flow,
Fragments scattered, seeds we sow.

A heart that wanders seeks to find,
The links that tether and unwind.
Through vibrant markets, dusk till dawn,
The world unfolds in tapestry drawn.

Lost in thoughts, I chase the light,
Each shadow speaks in silence tight.
From valleys low to peaks afar,
In every view, a hidden star.

In corners quaint, with strangers met,
Moments shared, we'll not forget.
A laugh, a smile, a shared refrain,
In fleeting time, we break the chain.

So take these fragments, hold them tight,
In every sunset, find the light.
For every journey, in heart's embrace,
Maps out a world of endless grace.

Through the Mist of Possibility

In the dawn of dreams we rise,
Veils of fog before our eyes.
Whispers call from paths unseen,
Beckoning through realms serene.

Hearts adorned with hopes and fears,
Navigating through silent years.
Each decision a gentle sway,
Guiding us along the way.

In the hush of morning light,
New horizons take their flight.
Every step a choice we make,
Through the mist, our fates awake.

With every turn, the world unfolds,
Stories waiting to be told.
In this dance of chance and time,
We find beauty in the climb.

Embrace the shadows, seek the glow,
In this journey, let love flow.
Through the mist, let visions soar,
In possibility, forevermore.

Bridges We Cross Along the Way

Underneath the arching skies,
We build our bridges, rise and rise.
Each connection holds a truth,
Carved from laughter, love, and youth.

Over rivers deep and wide,
We cross together, side by side.
Bound by dreams, we take the lead,
Nurtured by the seeds we heed.

With every step, foundations grow,
Stone by stone, the heart will know.
Though storms may rage and shadows fall,
Together we can conquer all.

Through valleys dark and mountains high,
We forge the paths, and never shy.
Hand in hand, we face the tide,
In every moment, love our guide.

At sunset's glow, our bridges gleam,
Mirrors of our hopes and dreams.
Together, we shall journey on,
Creating beauty, until dawn.

Unraveled Threads of Adventure

In the fabric of the night,
Stories woven, bold and bright.
Threads of fate, they intertwine,
Leading hearts toward the divine.

Each adventure, a different hue,
Colors brush the sky anew.
Through the chaos and the cheer,
Every step, we draw them near.

With the compass of our hearts,
Navigating through life's arts.
In the tapestry we weave,
Find the magic we believe.

Beneath the stars, we chase the thrill,
Every moment, our dreams fulfill.
With laughter echoing, we roam,
In uncharted lands, we find home.

As adventures unfold their wings,
In the silence, the heart sings.
Together, we embrace the chase,
In unraveled threads, we find our place.

Serene Moments on the Road

On the winding path we tread,
Soft whispers of the day ahead.
In stillness, find a joyful sound,
As nature's peace wraps all around.

Beneath the shade of ancient trees,
Time slows down, we feel the breeze.
With gentle eyes, we take it in,
Moments cherished, where love begins.

Each horizon, a promise near,
With every mile, we shed our fear.
In the quiet, our souls connect,
Serene beauty we won't neglect.

As the sun sets, colors blend,
Every journey leads to a friend.
In tranquil spaces, hearts unite,
Guided by the stars at night.

In these moments, life reveals,
The depth of joy that time conceals.
On the road, together we wander,
In serene moments, we grow fonder.

Rustic Dreams and Endless Roads

In the fields where shadows blend,
The whispers of the breeze descend.
Dusty trails lead far away,
To where the bright new dawn holds sway.

The sun dips low, the colors flare,
Each moment held, a tender care.
Footsteps trace the earth so kind,
In that road, our hopes entwined.

Nature's song, a tranquil hum,
Calls us back where dreams become.
With every turn, a tale unfolds,
Of rustic dreams and roads of gold.

Stars emerge in velvet skies,
While crickets serenade goodbyes.
Together here, hand in hand,
We wander through this endless land.

So let the journey greet our hearts,
As we embrace what life imparts.
On endless roads, where souls convene,
We find the spaces in between.

Selves Shaped by Valleys

In valleys deep where rivers flow,
The seeds of change begin to grow.
Mountains watch with ancient eyes,
Where silence breathes and wisdom lies.

Beneath the boughs that arch so wide,
We wander forth, our fears to bide.
Each echo holds a story dear,
Of who we are and what we steer.

Seasons shift, and time reveals,
The hidden paths that fate conceals.
With every step, we shape our fate,
In valleys wide, we contemplate.

The laughter shared, the tears we shed,
Crafts the person within our head.
Through trials faced, we come to see,
The selves we forge, the way we'll be.

So let the valleys guide our way,
In shadows cast where we can play.
With open hearts, we'll journey far,
To find the light beneath each star.

Reflections in Still Waters

In quiet pools where silence dwells,
The mirrored sky with secrets tells.
Ripples dance on gentle streams,
Reflecting all our hidden dreams.

A world unfolds in vibrant hues,
Painting stories with every muse.
We peer within, our thoughts in flow,
Where deep desires start to grow.

Leaves drift down, a soft embrace,
Each moment finds its sacred space.
In stillness, peace becomes the guide,
As time itself begins to glide.

The sun dips low, a golden hue,
In tranquil depths, we find what's true.
Amidst the calm, our hearts align,
With nature's pulse, we intertwine.

So seek the waters, deep and wide,
Let echoes of your soul reside.
In reflections clear, we grasp the grace,
Of life's great dance, our sacred place.

Unscripted Chapters

Each page unwritten waits for ink,
Where every thought leads us to think.
Moments woven, wild and free,
In unscripted tales, we find our plea.

With laughter shared, and tears aligned,
We carve our paths, with hearts unconfined.
Chasing dreams that dare to soar,
Opening every unfamiliar door.

Mistakes embraced, we learn to grow,
In stories told, our spirits glow.
With every turn, the plot may twist,
Yet through it all, we still persist.

New beginnings wait just down the lane,
Emerging brightly from joy and pain.
Every chapter, a dance of fate,
Unscripted lives we celebrate.

So pen the lines with courage bold,
In tales of warmth where hearts unfold.
In living pages, love will steer,
Our unscripted journeys, crystal clear.

In the Wake of Ephemeral Days

Soft whispers fade in twilight's glow,
A fleeting breeze through the willow's bow.
Moments like shadows drift and dance,
In the wake of time's fleeting glance.

Laughter echoes, then fades away,
Each heartbeat marks the close of day.
Yet in brief encounters, wonders reside,
Memories cherished, where dreams abide.

The sun dips low, a crimson tide,
With every ending, new paths collide.
Days may be short, but love remains,
In ephemeral beauty, hope sustains.

Glimmers of joy in the passing hour,
Petals unfold, revealing their power.
Nature's embrace, a gentle sigh,
In the wake of days that quickly fly.

So treasure the spark of each moment's breath,
In whispers of life, find sweetness in death.
For in the ephemeral, truth finds its way,
In the wake of ephemeral days, we'll stay.

Sketches of the Wandering Mind

A canvas filled with hues of thought,
Each stroke a glimpse of battles fought.
Wandering whispers, ideas take flight,
Sketches illuminated in the night.

Thoughts meander like rivers flow,
In the stillness, seeds of dreams grow.
Fragments of tales, both far and wide,
In the heart's corner, secrets confide.

The curious dance of shadows and light,
In the mind's garden, a beautiful sight.
Moments captured, a fleeting glance,
Sketches of life weave a mystic dance.

Pages unfold, with stories untold,
Dreams and realities, a tapestry bold.
A labyrinth of wonders, both near and far,
To navigate by the light of a star.

So let your thoughts paint the skies high,
In sketches of wonder, let your heart fly.
For the wandering mind, a boundless sea,
In every sketch, a pathway to be.

The Journey is the Destination

Each step we take along the way,
The journey unfolds, come what may.
Every twist and turn, a lesson learned,
In the dance of time, our spirits yearned.

Mountains conquered, valleys crossed,
In moments gained, we seldom lost.
For in the moving, the heart grows wise,
The journey, a gift in time's disguise.

Dreams on the horizon, silent calls,
In the echoes of adventure, the spirit sprawls.
With every mile, the soul ignites,
In the journey, our true heart writes.

Like rivers flowing to the endless sea,
Each path we wander shapes who we be.
The road ahead, a promise, a chance,
In the journey's essence, life's true dance.

So embrace the road, let worries fade,
For the journey is the legacy made.
With open arms and hearts set free,
In every step, the destination be.

Navigating the Labyrinth of Life

In the maze of dreams, we wander far,
Seeking truth beneath a silver star.
Twisting corridors, shadows cast,
In the labyrinth, memories amassed.

Choices lay like stones in a stream,
Reflecting hopes, igniting a dream.
In every turn, a lesson learned,
Navigating paths that fate has turned.

Moments of doubt, the heart will steer,
Through whispered fears, love will appear.
In the tangled web of joy and strife,
We find our way, embracing life.

With courage found in the darkest night,
Stars guide us onward, a flickering light.
In the labyrinth, we grow and rise,
Through trials faced, we reach the skies.

So trust the journey, however rife,
In the dance of fate, we find our life.
Navigate boldly, let your spirit thrive,
In the labyrinth of life, we truly arrive.

A Voyage Through Vistas

In the dawn's soft embrace, we sail,
Past the mountains, through the vale.
Colors dance in the waking light,
Guiding dreams in their flight.

Waves whisper secrets of lands unknown,
Every crest, a new story sown.
The horizon calls with a gentle hand,
As we journey to a distant land.

Breezes carry scents of the sea,
Echoes of laughter, wild and free.
Clouds gather like thoughts in the mind,
In this voyage, treasures we find.

Stars emerge as the sun takes rest,
In the night sky, our hopes expressed.
Oceans stretch, vast and wide,
On this canvas, we take pride.

With every wave, we grow and learn,
For in the journey, our hearts yearn.
Together we chase, together we roam,
In the vistas, we find our home.

The Road Less Traveled

In the quiet woods, a path unfolds,
Where stories linger, waiting to be told.
Footprints of those who dared to stray,
In the whispers, they show the way.

Sunlight dapples the forest floor,
Every step a chance to explore.
Through tangled vines and shadows deep,
Into the wild, memories to keep.

Rustling leaves share ancient lore,
With each breath, we yearn for more.
Every bend holds a promise bright,
In the twilight, our souls take flight.

Climb the hills, view the terrain,
Embrace the joy, withstand the pain.
For in the choices we dare to make,
The bonds we forge, never to break.

In the embrace of nature's call,
We find our strength, we rise, we fall.
On this road where few have tread,
We weave our dreams, in heart and head.

Tales of the Unseen Mile

Over the hills, a tale entwined,
With secrets held and hopes confined.
Every step forges a new refrain,
In the distance, whispers of gain.

The air is thick with stories old,
Of paths less walked, of hearts so bold.
With courage stitched in every seam,
We chase the echoes of a dream.

Through laughter lost and tears regained,
In the journey, our spirits trained.
Each unseen mile brings us near,
To the heartbeats of those we hold dear.

As dusk descends and shadows creep,
We gather warmth, our souls to keep.
In every heartbeat, a rhythm fine,
Tales unfold, beautifully divine.

With eyes wide open, we seek the light,
In unseen miles, we find our sight.
The journey's truth, a precious file,
Embracing life, every unseen mile.

Breathing in New Horizons

In the morning mist, our spirits rise,
Chasing dreams beneath endless skies.
Each horizon whispers a promise bright,
Inviting us to new realms of light.

With every breath, the world unfolds,
In vibrant colors, new stories told.
The air is fresh with hope and thrill,
As we journey forth, guided by will.

Mountains loom with a gentle grace,
Tempering fears we long to face.
Across valleys vast, we'll dare to roam,
For in each step, we carve our home.

Together we face the unknown seas,
With laughter carried on the breeze.
In this dance of chance and fate,
We open our hearts and celebrate.

With eyes aflame, we seek to soar,
Beyond the limits we knew before.
For in the depths of a new sunrise,
We breathe in life, embracing skies.

The Colors of the Path Ahead

Red like the dawn, bright and bold,
Green of the leaves, stories untold.
Blue like the skies, endless and wide,
Yellow of hope, a warm, sunny guide.

Orange of autumn, a fiery embrace,
Purple of twilight, a gentle grace.
Each color a promise, each step we take,
Painting our journey, for our own sake.

In shades of the past, our dreams intertwine,
With confidence blooming, like a soft vine.
As we walk the path, steadfast and true,
The colors of life shine bright for me and you.

A Dance with Destiny

Two souls entwined, a rhythm begins,
With every heartbeat, the magic spins.
Footsteps in harmony, echo through time,
A melody written, in whispers and rhyme.

Stars above twinkle, guiding our way,
As we twirl in the night, come what may.
Every stumble a chance, each fall a new rise,
In this dance of fate, we learn to be wise.

Caught in the moment, we sway and we glide,
With courage as our partner, we'll never hide.
Embracing the future, we embrace the now,
A beautiful journey, to which we say vow.

The Spirit of Moving Forward

With every sunset, a promise we keep,
In the shadows of doubt, our spirits leap.
Carving a path with determination strong,
The rhythm of progress sings our sweet song.

Mountains we climb, valleys we cross,
Learning from trials, never a loss.
With hearts as our compass, we steer clear of fear,
For tomorrow holds treasures, bright and near.

Resilience our armor, we step into light,
Driven by passions, igniting the night.
The spirit of moving forward, ever so true,
Embracing the journey, in all that we do.

Unearthed Treasures of Experience

Beneath the surface, gems lie in wait,
Stories of journeys, wisdom, and fate.
With every lesson, we dig, we find,
Unearthed treasures that sharpen the mind.

Golden memories shine from the past,
Tales of resilience, shadows cast.
Embracing the trials that molded our soul,
As we gather strength, we become whole.

Time weaves its magic, a tapestry bright,
Each thread is a moment, a spark of insight.
In life's hidden corners, we learn to believe,
Unearthed treasures inspire us to achieve.

Waves of Transience

The ocean breathes in silent sighs,
While moonlight drapes the restless tide.
Moments flicker, then they fade,
Like whispered dreams in twilight's keep.

Seashells whisper tales of time,
Carried far on currents wide.
Each wave a rhythm of goodbye,
And echoes of what once was here.

Beneath the surface, secrets sleep,
In depths where shadows drift and glide.
Yet every crest brings forth new life,
In cycles wrought by nature's hand.

Hold dear the paths the waters weave,
For fleeting is the shore we stand.
With every splash, with every draw,
We learn to cherish, let things go.

In sweetness found and sorrow felt,
We ride the tides, we part, we grow.
The waves remind us to embrace,
The beauty in what slips away.

Unfolding Maps

Ink spills on the wrinkled page,
Where dreams and paths collide in ink.
Each curve, a choice yet unmade,
Each line a journey into the unknown.

Mountains rise in distant view,
Valleys cradle the wandering soul.
With each compass sway and turn,
New stories laid beneath our feet.

Footprints fade with passing days,
Yet traces linger in the mind.
A landscape changes, softly fades,
While new horizons come to light.

Maps are more than ink and lines,
They chart the heart's uncertain quest.
Through forests deep and rivers wide,
We find ourselves in every step.

With every fold and every crease,
The world reveals its hidden dreams.
We wander on, through night and day,
As maps unfold like timeless tales.

Dancing with Uncertainty

Steps uncertain on the floor,
Where shadows twist and moments pause.
In every leap, a breath of doubt,
Yet beauty blooms within the risk.

Whispers of the night surround,
In silence, echoes make their call.
We sway to rhythms of the heart,
A dance of life, both fierce and free.

Gripping tight, then letting go,
We twirl through fear, we laugh in grace.
In fleeting seconds, joy ignites,
As we consume the unknown's fire.

Each misstep becomes a lesson,
Each stumble draws a knowing smile.
With open arms, we greet the dawn,
Where uncertainty joins the dance.

To live is to embrace the thrill,
To dive into the wild unknown.
So dance with me, take my hand,
In this bright maze we will explore.

The Art of Wandering

Footprints scattered on the trail,
A path unwritten, wild and free.
In every breath, a story breathes,
In every turn, the world unfolds.

The call of distant lands invites,
A whisper born from ancient dust.
What lies beyond each bend and rise?
A secret wrapped in mystery's hand.

With each step, the heart ignites,
Curiosity our guiding light.
In meadows bright and valleys deep,
We find the art of being lost.

The road may wander, curve, or stray,
Yet beauty sparkles in the stray.
Through forests dense and mountains steep,
Adventure beckons, come what may.

For wandering is not a course,
But finding joy in every chance.
With every pause, we learn to see,
The world reveals its wondrous dance.

The Canvas of Life

Upon the canvas, colors blend,
Brushstrokes bold, as dreams extend.
Every hue, a tale to tell,
In vibrant worlds where hopes dwell.

Strokes of joy, and shades of pain,
Layered stories, love's sweet gain.
Fleeting moments, captured bright,
Each canvas holds a piece of light.

Ebbing tides of chance and fate,
Create the scenes that we await.
With every swirl, a journey grows,
In life's own frame, resilience shows.

Palette rich with laughter, tears,
Crafting visions through the years.
A portrait of both loss and grace,
In colors bold, we find our place.

As time unveils its final art,
The canvas speaks of every heart.
A masterpiece of life revealed,
In strokes of love, we are healed.

Shadows and Sunlight

Dancing shadows on the wall,
Chasing dreams, we rise and fall.
Sunlight whispers through the trees,
Nature's song, a gentle breeze.

In twilight's glow, the world transforms,
Beneath the stars, a heart conforms.
Light and dark, they intertwine,
Crafting paths where fate aligns.

Every shadow holds a story,
Echoing whispers of forgotten glory.
Sunlight breaks, dispelling fears,
In this dance of days and years.

Through the night, the shadows creep,
Guarding secrets that we keep.
Yet the dawn will always rise,
Chasing clouds from painted skies.

In the balance of dark and light,
We find our way, embracing night.
With every step, a choice we make,
Shadows and sunlight, paths awake.

Embracing the Twilight

As daylight fades, a quiet hush,
The sun retreats, the skies a blush.
Stars awaken, softly gleam,
In twilight's arms, we dare to dream.

Colors blend in a fading light,
Night unveils its velvet sight.
Crickets sing in harmony,
Nature's night-time symphony.

Within this hour, all feels right,
Hearts aligned in the cool twilight.
Whispers shared beneath the moon,
A promise held to linger soon.

Shadows lengthen, yet hope ignites,
In the mélange of days and nights.
We embrace the calm, the serene,
In twilight's glow, our souls convene.

As stars twinkle in the dark,
Every journey finds its spark.
With open arms, we greet the night,
Embracing dreams that take to flight.

The Tapestry of Destiny

Woven threads of fate we find,
In patterns rich and intertwined.
Every strand, a life embraced,
In colors bright, our dreams are laced.

Choices made, like needle's poke,
Crafting tales that weave and stoke.
Each moment sown with care and grace,
An intricate dance, a timeless space.

In this tapestry, love prevails,
Binding hearts through joys and trails.
While shadows may attempt to bind,
Light will always seek to find.

As stories cross and paths conjoin,
Destiny sings, a sweet adjoin.
Finding solace in the weave,
Trusting what we can achieve.

In patterns vast, we search for truth,
The tapestry holds the soul of youth.
Embrace the threads, both strong and frayed,
For in this fabric, dreams are made.

Dance of the Open Road

Wheels roll gently on the earth,
Beneath the sun, a dance begins.
The wind whispers tales of freedom,
As horizons draw me in again.

Each mile a story yet untold,
With laughter echoing in the breeze.
Mountains rise, rivers run bold,
And my heart finds joy with ease.

The asphalt shimmers in the light,
Guiding dreams along the way.
Footsteps light, futures bright,
In every turn, new hopes will play.

Stars appear as daylight fades,
In twilight's embrace, I am found.
With every journey fear evades,
Adventure's song is all around.

So let me roam where roads unfold,
Chasing sunsets, chasing stars.
In every step, my spirit's bold,
The open road, my heart's memoirs.

Echoes of Tomorrow's Dream

In silent nights, the whispers rise,
A world of thoughts, a maze of schemes.
Each shadow hints of future ties,
As mind drifts into woven dreams.

Tomorrow calls with soft, sweet grace,
Its echoes dance on twilight's breath.
Hope's familiar, warm embrace,
Whispers secrets beyond death.

We chase the dawn with open eyes,
For every step holds mystery.
In darkness, light will find its prize,
Tomorrow blooms in history.

Voices linger in gentle song,
Reminding us of paths we've crossed.
In unity, we all belong,
No dream too big, no dream too lost.

So rise with me, let dreams converge,
In harmony, our spirits soar.
As tomorrows beckon, feel the urge,
To chase the whispers evermore.

Finding Solace in the Steps

With every footfall on the ground,
A rhythm builds beneath the sky.
In quiet places, peace I've found,
Where echoes of the world drift by.

The path may twist, the road may bend,
Yet solace waits in simple ways.
Within each stride, our hearts can mend,
As nature sings in soothing lays.

The crunch of leaves beneath my shoes,
A heartbeat synced with earth's soft hum.
In every step, a life I choose,
With every breath, new songs will come.

In solitude, I mend the seams,
Of weary thoughts and restless hearts.
With every journey, feed the dreams,
Embrace the now as past departs.

So let me wander, let me roam,
In steps so sacred, find my peace.
With every path, I create a home,
As worries fade and troubles cease.

The Map Written in Stars

Upon the canvas of the night,
Constellations gleam like dreams.
Each twinkle tells a tale of flight,
A journey traced in silver beams.

The Milky Way, a river wide,
Carries whispers from afar.
In stardust paths, our hopes abide,
A guiding light, our northern star.

Lost in thoughts beneath the glow,
Each star a spark of what could be.
With every gaze, the heart will know,
The universe has set us free.

Galaxies swirl, their secrets glow,
In cosmic dance, we find our place.
With every pulse, the ancients show,
The map of dreams in night's soft grace.

So let me wander 'neath the sky,
In awe of all that's yet to come.
With every wish, I'll learn to fly,
For in these stars, my heart finds home.

The Canvas of Uncharted Seas

Waves whisper softly to the shore,
A horizon painted with hopes galore.
Every swell a mystery yet to find,
In the depths of blue, we leave time behind.

Sails billow wide, catching the breeze,
The stars guide us through the night with ease.
Every star a wish, every wave a song,
In this vast expanse, we know we belong.

The sun dips low, spilling gold on the tide,
In the dance of the sea, our dreams collide.
No maps chart the wonders we have seen,
Across the canvas, we craft our serene.

From hidden coves to the jagged cliffs,
The voyage teaches us its own gifts.
Each splash of water, each gust of wind,
Adds color and depth to the journey we begin.

In the heart of the ocean, whispers ignite,
As our spirits soar beneath the moonlight.
This canvas unfolds with each passing day,
A masterpiece born on the waves' ballet.

Threads That Create Our Tale

We weave our stories on a loom of time,
Each moment a stitch, each breath a rhyme.
Threads of laughter, and threads of pain,
In the tapestry of life, all threads remain.

Colors vivid, some dull, others bright,
Each hue tells a story of joy and fright.
Interwoven patterns, sharp and unique,
Creating a story only we can speak.

The hands that sew are guided by fate,
Crafting our tale, it's never too late.
With every knot tied, a memory held,
In the fabric of life, our truths are spelled.

As seasons change, so does our weave,
In every unraveling, more to believe.
The threads connect us, across the years,
Binding our hearts, through laughter and tears.

In this quilt of existence, we surely find,
The love and the pain, intricately aligned.
Threads that create what we cherish and share,
In the weft and the warp, we discover our care.

Reflections Along the Way

Mirrors of nature, deep lakes so clear,
Reflecting the dreams of what we hold dear.
In stillness, we ponder the paths we have taken,
Every ripple a memory, never forsaken.

Sunlight dances on water's embrace,
Illuminating thoughts with warmth and grace.
The journey unfolds in the calm and the storm,
Through reflections, our spirits transform.

Mountains loom tall, casting shadows so wide,
In their presence, we find solace inside.
With every ascent, we learn and we grow,
In reflections, our past softly glows.

Each step we take leaves a mark along the way,
In the heart's mirror, we'll find what to say.
Embracing the echoes of laughter and sighs,
In the silence of thought, our true self lies.

Reflections remind us of who we have been,
The beauty in flaws, the strength within.
As we carry on, with strength and dismay,
In each shimmering glance, life's truths stay.

A Journey Woven with Dreams

In the quiet of night, dreams softly unfurl,
Like whispers of secrets, they twirl and whirl.
Each vision a pathway, winding and clear,
In the fabric of hope, we cast off our fear.

Stars above guide our hearts on the way,
Illuminating wishes that silently sway.
Through valleys of doubt and mountains of trust,
We weave our desires from passion and dust.

With every heartbeat, new dreams arise,
Painting the canvas of endless skies.
In the dance of the night, we seek to explore,
Each woven intention invites us for more.

Through laughter and tears, together we strive,
In the tapestry of life, we truly thrive.
Every moment a stitch, in harmony seams,
A journey unfolds, woven with dreams.

So here we embark, with hope as our thread,
The future awaits, where visions are led.
Together we'll journey, hand in hand, we roam,
In this woven adventure, we'll always find home.

Footprints in the Sand

As waves recede, the footprints fade,
Memories linger where we once played.
Each step a story, soft and grand,
Eternity marked in grains of sand.

The sun sets low, a golden hue,
Whispers of journeys that we once knew.
In the twilight, shadows blend,
Footprints remain, but time won't mend.

The tides return, erasing the past,
Yet in my heart, those moments last.
With every wave, a promise stands,
Forever etched, those footprints in sands.

In solitude, I walk alone,
Reflecting on paths that I have grown.
Yet with each step under skies so wide,
I carry the footprints deep inside.

As dawn breaks anew, the world awakes,
In every dawn, another chance makes.
The footprints tell, a tale so true,
In the sands of time, I walk anew.

A Symphony of Choices

In every heartbeat, choices play,
A melody composed each day.
Harmonic whispers guide the soul,
As we embark on paths made whole.

The notes of life, both sharp and sweet,
Echo through halls where dreams compete.
A symphony builds, rich and rare,
With every choice, the air we share.

In quiet moments, chords arise,
Crafted by hands, beneath the skies.
Each choice a note, a line we write,
Creating harmony in day and night.

With crescendos loud, the silence breaks,
In choice, the beauty of risk awakes.
A dance of fate, with rhythms bold,
In this symphony, our lives unfold.

Through time, we play, a vibrant score,
Adding layers, seeking more.
Every choice, a step toward our dreams,
In this grand symphony, nothing's as it seems.

The Compass of the Heart

Silent whispers guide our way,
Through the night and into day.
With every beat, the compass turns,
A flame inside, forever burns.

In tangled woods and distant shores,
The heart recalls what it adores.
In trials faced, through joy and pain,
The compass points to love's refrain.

Through stormy skies and paths unknown,
The heart reveals what must be sown.
With love as guide, we find our place,
In the vast expanse of time and space.

Every longing, every sigh,
Is a direction, a reason why.
Trust the compass, follow the spark,
In shadows bright, reveal the dark.

As seasons change and years go by,
The compass leads, it cannot lie.
With each decision, trust the art,
Navigate life with the compass of heart.

Navigating Dreams

In quiet corners of the mind,
Dreams emerge and intertwine.
With whispered hopes, we take our flight,
Navigating through the starry night.

Each dream a map, a guiding star,
Remote destinations, near and far.
With heart as sailor and will as breeze,
We chart our course through endless seas.

The waves may crash, the winds may shift,
Yet dreams persist, a sacred gift.
Through storms we learn, we grow, we see,
Navigating to who we can be.

In every setback, a lesson keen,
In every challenge, horizons seen.
The heart, the compass, the soul, the ship,
In dreams we trust as we boldly skip.

As dawn approaches, dreams awake,
In every heartbeat, choices make.
Navigating paths, we find our way,
In the tapestry of night and day.

Shadows of the Journey Ahead

In the stillness of the night,
Shadows whisper, tales of light.
Paths untrodden, dreams yet spun,
Hopes awaken, journeys begun.

Footsteps echo, fears untold,
Through the dark, courage unfolds.
Each turn holds an unseen grace,
With every stride, we find our place.

Voices linger, soft and near,
Guiding hearts with gentle cheer.
In the twilight, visions blend,
The horizon calls us to transcend.

Mountains high, valleys deep,
In the silence, secrets keep.
Through the shadows, we shall roam,
Finding solace, crafting home.

With each dawn, the past we shed,
Into the light, our spirits led.
Together we'll rise, hand in hand,
Chasing dreams across this land.

Finding Light in the Turns

Winding paths, we lose our way,
Yet the dawn brings hope each day.
Through the fog, a glimmer shows,
Guiding us where the river flows.

Every twist, a lesson learned,
Burning bright, our passions churned.
Even in shadows, love ignites,
Turning darkness into lights.

Steps are heavy, burdens vast,
But the light, it holds us fast.
In the chaos, purpose gleams,
Mending hearts and broken dreams.

Through the storms, we find our way,
Every night fades into day.
Every heartbeat builds the bridge,
Leading us beyond the ridge.

With your hand inside of mine,
Every turn, our hearts entwine.
In the journey, truths unfold,
Light our path, and make us whole.

Landscapes of the Soul

In tranquil fields, our spirits play,
Where thoughts like wildflowers sway.
Mountains rise, a mighty tale,
In every breeze, the whispers sail.

Rivers of time carve memories deep,
In silent valleys, secrets keep.
Every sunrise paints the sky,
With strokes of hope as dreams fly high.

From the peaks, the world unfolds,
Stories of life, courage bold.
In every sunset's warm embrace,
We find peace, a sacred space.

Through shifting sands, we learn to roam,
Each landscape weaving threads of home.
Stars above, guiding light,
Illuminating the quiet night.

With every heartbeat, we explore,
Landscapes vast, forevermore.
In the souls we meet and share,
Beauty blooms, everywhere.

The Call of Distant Shores

Waves crash softly on the sand,
Echoes calling from afar, grand.
Whispers of a journey new,
Inviting hearts, both brave and true.

Sails unfurl, the wind will guide,
Through uncharted seas, we'll glide.
With each promise, dreams will swell,
In the depths, our stories dwell.

Tides will shift, yet we remain,
In the storms, we'll dance with rain.
Every horizon, a new chance,
The heart takes flight in wild dance.

Stars will chart our course at night,
Each spark a flicker of pure light.
To distant shores, we'll make our way,
With courage born in every sway.

Together we'll roam, find the true,
In every moment, start anew.
The call of shores beyond the foam,
In our hearts, we'll always roam.

The Canvas of a Wandering Heart

Upon the road where dreams take flight,
 Colors blend in the soft twilight.
Each step a brush, each thought a hue,
 Painting life with shades so true.

Whispers of winds through ancient trees,
 Carry tales on a gentle breeze.
Fleeting moments like clouds above,
 Outline a journey, shaped by love.

Stars awaken as shadows play,
 Guiding souls who roam and sway.
In the stillness, find the art,
 Sketching silence, a wandering heart.

Paths that cross, then drift apart,
 Each connection, a work of heart.
Embracing every twist and turn,
 In every loss, there's much to learn.

With every dawn, the canvas glows,
 Infinite tales the wanderer knows.
Brush strokes bold, yet gentle, fine,
 Life's masterpiece, a path divine.

While the World Unfolds

Amidst the hustle of daily grind,
Nature waits with a voice so kind.
Secrets hid in every leaf,
The pulse of life, both sweet and brief.

Moments linger like morning dew,
Glistening bright, a frame anew.
Beneath the sky, the shadows shift,
Time weaves tales, a precious gift.

As sunset paints the land in gold,
Silent stories of old unfold.
Memories breathe in whispered tones,
Nature's heart, our own, it hones.

With every twilight's tender gaze,
Is found the spark of new-found ways.
In stillness, wisdom starts to rise,
While the world unfolds, we realize.

So take a breath, let worries cease,
In nature's arms, we find our peace.
Together journey, hand in hand,
As life's collage colors the land.

In Tune with the Traveling Song

Across the mountains, valleys wide,
Echoes of laughter, stars as guide.
Each note a thread, each chord a dream,
Life unfolds, a melodic theme.

Whistling winds in harmony call,
For the dreamers who long to sprawl.
In every beat, a story told,
Adventures that never grow old.

As rivers dance to the sun's warm light,
Our hearts entwined in a joyous flight.
Footsteps align to the rhythm's pace,
Chasing echoes, we find our place.

From bustling streets to quiet glens,
Harmony thrives in the journey's bends.
With every sigh, we sing along,
Hearts in sync with the traveling song.

So let the chorus of life resound,
In every heartbeat, love is found.
As we gather notes from every start,
We'll dance forever, hand in heart.

Chasing the Horizon's Edge

Where the sky kisses the ocean's blue,
Sunsets paint a promise, bold and true.
We chase the dreams that stretch so wide,
Fearless and free, we take the ride.

Across the fields, where wildflowers bloom,
The scent of adventure breaks the gloom.
With every sunrise, our spirits soar,
Endless journeys, we long for more.

Through valleys deep and mountains high,
We follow trails beneath the sky.
In every whisper of wind that flies,
There lies the secret of the wise.

With hope in hand, we wander far,
Each moment a treasure, each step a star.
Unfurling paths ignite our souls,
In pursuit of dreams, we become whole.

So let us chase what lies ahead,
Brave the storms, defy the dread.
For life is a canvas, vast and wide,
Chasing the horizon's edge, we glide.

Soaring into the Vastness

Wings spread wide, I rise up high,
Chasing dreams across the sky.
Clouds embrace my flight so free,
Whispers of the wind call me.

Beneath the sun, I dance and glide,
Through the open, endless tide.
Mountains bow to greet my view,
Nature's canvas, vast and true.

Stars will guide my way at night,
In the dark, they shine so bright.
The universe is mine to roam,
In the vastness, I find home.

With each breath, I feel alive,
In the skies, my spirit thrives.
Freedom sings in every beat,
Soaring high, my heart's retreat.

Seeds of a New Beginning

In the earth, a promise lies,
Tiny seeds beneath the skies.
Nurtured by the sun's warm glow,
Hope awakens, starts to grow.

Gentle rains will calm the ground,
Life emerges, fresh and sound.
Roots dig deep, reach for the light,
In the darkness, blooms the bright.

Time will dance, the seasons change,
Colors shift, the world, arrange.
Petals fold and then unfold,
Every story yet untold.

From the struggle, beauty thrives,
In this garden, spirit strives.
With each breath, new life we bring,
Seeds of hope, our hearts shall sing.

Rivers of Reflection

Flowing softly, water gleams,
Carving paths through silent dreams.
Mirrors hold the sky's embrace,
Nature's whispers in this space.

Each ripple tells a story grand,
Of distant shores and foreign lands.
Time flows gently, never still,
In these waters, hearts can fill.

Sunrise breaks upon the stream,
Casting light on all we dream.
Reflections dance on liquid glass,
Moments cherished, swift to pass.

Beneath the surface, secrets hide,
Echoes of the past reside.
In solitude, we seek our way,
Through the rivers, we shall sway.

The Heart's Expedition

Inward journeys, paths unknown,
Searching for the seeds I've sown.
Wanderlust within my chest,
Yearning for this questing rest.

Mountains rise, a test in height,
Every step, a dance of light.
Through the valleys, shadows play,
Guiding me along the way.

With each heartbeat, stories unfold,
Secrets kept, and dreams retold.
Emotions chart the course I find,
On this voyage, soul entwined.

Bridges built from trust and care,
Connections bloom in the fresh air.
Navigating love's embrace,
In the heart, I find my place.

The Dance of Uncertainty

In shadows where whispers weave,
Footsteps falter, hearts believe.
A path unclear, yet we will tread,
With dreams alive and fears widespread.

The night sways gently with the breeze,
Unraveling doubts like autumn leaves.
In every twirl, a question spun,
In every pause, a rising sun.

The world a canvas, colors blend,
With each new step, we start to mend.
In the chaos, clarity grows,
A dance of chance, where courage flows.

We sway to music, soft and low,
With heartbeats racing, we let go.
Embracing doubt as part of cheer,
In every misstep, we draw near.

So take my hand, together we'll prance,
In this wild and fearless dance.
Through uncertainty, we shall find,
The joy that blooms within the blind.

Lost and Found

In the corners of dusty rooms,
Whispers echo, hidden glooms.
Faded photos, stories old,
Of lives once lived, of dreams retold.

Amongst the shadows, treasures lie,
Forgotten hopes that never die.
In what we lose, we also gain,
A tapestry of joy and pain.

Hands reach for what they wish to seize,
In cracks of time, we find our ease.
Each moment lost is not in vain,
For in the search, we feel the rain.

Through tangled paths of heart and mind,
We weave new tales, the past entwined.
In every tear, a lesson found,
In every smile, love has abound.

So cherish the chaos, the paired divide,
For lost and found walk side by side.
In journeys deep, in hearts we hold,
Life's truths emerge, like gems of gold.

In the Footsteps of Stars

Underneath a velvet sky,
We chase the dreams that glitter high.
In constellations, stories glowed,
Guiding us on the paths we've sowed.

With every breath, a wish ignites,
In secret realms of endless nights.
Stardust whispers, calling near,
Encouraging hearts to persevere.

Through cosmic dances, we shall roam,
In the light of stars, we find our home.
With every glance, the heavens speak,
In twinkling brightness, futures peek.

We walk the trails where stardust falls,
In gentle murmurs, the universe calls.
Holding tight to the magic spun,
In the footsteps of stars, we run.

So let us leap beyond the bar,
Forever drawn by the evening star.
In every heartbeat, an echo flows,
In the dance of fate, our spirit grows.

The Quest for Belonging

In the maze of faces, we search for home,
In every stranger, we dare to roam.
A tapestry woven with threads of care,
In laughter and sorrow, we find our share.

With open hearts, we reach and dare,
To bridge the gaps, to truly share.
In every hello, a spark ignites,
A promise of warmth in lonely nights.

Through valleys deep, through mountains high,
We seek connection, no reason why.
In every step, a story spun,
In the quest for love, we are all one.

A circle wide, both near and far,
In this grand journey, we're never ajar.
Together we'll weave a bond so strong,
In the quest for belonging, we all belong.

So let us gather, hands intertwined,
In the heart of the world, true peace we find.
With open arms, we chase the light,
In the quest for belonging, we reunite.

Storylines of the Uncharted

In whispers of the breeze they weave,
Tales of lands that few believe.
Each horizon hides a brand new quest,
Where dreams and wanderers find their rest.

Maps are inked with starlit glow,
Paths yet taken, seeds to sow.
With every step a story blooms,
In shadows deep where magic looms.

Curiosities beckon, heartbeats race,
Through tangled woods, we find our place.
The rhythm of the world aligns,
With every breath, a fate entwines.

Waves of time crash on the shore,
Tales of old that we explore.
Each horizon whispers soft and clear,
Guiding us where we hold most dear.

So we journey forth, hand in hand,
Across the sea, we make our stand.
In uncharted realms, we create our art,
Etching the tales of a fearless heart.

Pathways of the Heart

In the quiet moments, love is found,
In every whisper, a sacred sound.
With every heartbeat, feelings flow,
Like rivers winding, softly aglow.

Beneath the stars, in shadowed glade,
The dreams we share, the fears we trade.
Hand in hand, through night we roam,
Finding solace in the unknown.

Each path we tread, a tale unfolds,
Of laughter shared and stories told.
Through storms and sunshine, hearts entwine,
In every challenge, our spirits shine.

In the dance of time, we weave our fate,
With every moment, learning to wait.
Within the silence, love's hymn sings,
A melody that echoes through all things.

So here we stand, on love's grand stage,
Turning the world with every page.
In pathways winding, hand in hand,
Together we find where we both stand.

Unfolding Horizons

As dawn awakens with gentle light,
New horizons call, a wondrous sight.
With eyes wide open, we take the leap,
Into the unknown, our dreams to keep.

Mountains rise like guardians bold,
Stories within, waiting to unfold.
With each ascent, our spirits soar,
Boundless visions we can't ignore.

The oceans whisper secrets deep,
In waves of calm, the heart can weep.
Horizons stretch, where sky meets sea,
In moments still, we're truly free.

Paths of wonder lie ahead,
With every turn, new journeys spread.
In fields of gold, beneath the sun,
Together we'll chase what's just begun.

So let the winds of change embrace,
As we explore this sacred space.
With hearts wide open, we'll dare to roam,
Unfolding horizons, a world called home.

Steps on the Winding Road

On winding roads we find our way,
Through thick of woods, where shadows play.
Each step we take, a tale is spun,
In every footfall, journeys begun.

Beneath the canopy of emerald green,
The whispers of nature, softly seen.
In tangled paths, with courage bold,
We forge ahead, our stories told.

With every turn, the past we trace,
In memories held, a warm embrace.
As footprints fade, new ones appear,
On this winding road, we conquer fear.

Through seasons' change, we learn to flow,
In sunlit moments, our spirits glow.
We gather strength from roots so deep,
In every heartbeat, love we keep.

So take my hand as we stroll along,
Through winding paths, in nature's song.
In every step, our dreams are sown,
Together we walk, no longer alone.

Pathways of Solitude

In quiet woods where shadows play,
A single path leads me away.
The rustle of leaves, a gentle sigh,
In solitude's embrace, I fly.

A world untouched by hurried feet,
Where silence wraps me, bittersweet.
Each step I take, a whisper clear,
In this stillness, I draw near.

Sunlight filters through the trees,
Kissing the ground with tender ease.
A moment lost, yet found within,
In solitude, my heart can spin.

The echoes of my thoughts entwined,
With nature's pulse, I redefine.
Each moment stretched like tattered thread,
In peace, my worries gently tread.

I wander far from all I know,
To find the seeds of hope to sow.
In lonely streets, I learn to see,
The beauty there in being free.

The Wind in My Hair

As I ride upon the breeze,
Wild and free among the trees.
The world spins fast, a fleeting glance,
In the wind, I lose my chance.

With every gust, my spirit soars,
Across the hills, through open doors.
A gentle nudge, a playful dance,
In nature's arms, I find my chance.

The sky above a canvas wide,
A swirling blue, my heart's true guide.
The whispers of the past float near,
As the wind rushes, I feel no fear.

Moments steal like passing clouds,
Yet in this dance, my heart is proud.
With hair ablaze in sunlight's glow,
I am the wild, the brave, the flow.

The road ahead is vast and bright,
With every breeze, I greet the light.
So with the wind, my soul will share,
The secrets found in open air.

Whispers of the Road

Each mile I travel, secrets told,
In whispers soft, the journey unfolds.
With every bend, a story ignites,
Under the stars, through long, quiet nights.

Footsteps echo on the dusty trail,
Guiding my dreams, where hopes prevail.
The canvas sprawls of earth and sky,
In every heartbeat, spirits fly.

Through winding paths, the shadows play,
Where every whisper holds the day.
The call of far-off lands my muse,
Inviting me to always choose.

Worn out shoes tell tales of grace,
Each journey etched, a soft embrace.
As moonlight spills like melted cream,
The road whispers sweet, eternal dream.

So here I stand, at the crossroad's crest,
Finding peace within each quest.
In every silence, the road confides,
The whispers echo where freedom rides.

Steps into the Unknown

A path unfolds before my feet,
With every step, a brand-new beat.
The dark ahead, a canvas bare,
In shadows dense, I shed my care.

The heart whispers, 'dare to roam,'
In the unknown, I make my home.
Embracing fear, I take the dive,
To feel the pulse, to feel alive.

Uncharted trails call out my name,
With every turn, a chance to claim.
The future's fog, a soft embrace,
In the unknown, I find my place.

I thread my dreams through twilight's veil,
In every moment, I set sail.
With open arms for what will come,
Into the void, my heartbeats drum.

Each step that leads into the dark,
Ignites the spark, ignites the spark.
Though pathways twist and shadows grow,
In every ounce of doubt, I glow.

Miles of Revelation

In whispers soft, the road unfolds,
Beneath the sun, the story's told.
With every step, the world reveals,
The truth in silence, time conceals.

Mountains tower, shadows play,
A dance of light, both night and day.
Through valleys deep, the thoughts ignite,
In every corner, dreams take flight.

Rivers speak in lucid tones,
Carving paths through ancient stones.
The heartbeats echo, calm and pure,
In nature's lap, we find our cure.

With open eyes, we navigate,
The threads of fate, we contemplate.
Each mile a lesson, wisdom shared,
On roads of truth, we are prepared.

At journey's end, we stand anew,
With miles behind, the skies so blue.
In every moment, love's embrace,
Reveals the world, a sacred space.

A Journey Without Maps

Lost in time, we set our course,
With only dreams to guide our force.
The stars above, they point the way,
As night unfolds, we choose to stay.

Mountains high and valleys low,
Each step we take, the winds do blow.
With every twist, a tale we weave,
Through forests thick and webs believe.

The heart of earth beneath our feet,
In every pulse, the rhythm sweet.
With open arms, we greet the dawn,
A journey mapped on love withdrawn.

No compass guides, just trust inside,
Through rivers wide, we bravely ride.
Together hand in hand we roam,
A journey without maps, our home.

A fleeting glance at moments gone,
Our laughter echoes, bright as dawn.
In every trial, we grow and learn,
Each step we take, a flame does burn.

So here we stand, our spirits high,
With open hearts, we touch the sky.
A journey boundless, ever free,
In every breath, our mystery.

Where the Wild Things Lead

In restless dreams, the wild things call,
Through tangled woods where shadows fall.
With freedom's edge, we chase the night,
In whispers sweet, the stars ignite.

Through hidden paths, we find our way,
With open hearts, we dare to play.
With every roar, the silence breaks,
Where magic lives, and wonder wakes.

The moon will guide, the owls will sing,
As laughter dances on the wing.
Embrace the wild, let spirits soar,
Where every heartbeat begs for more.

In fields of gold, the wild things nest,
In untamed lands, we feel our best.
With open eyes, life's canvas speaks,
In every creak, the freedom leaks.

So join the dance, the rhythm wild,
In nature's arms, we're never mild.
With every step, the world we greet,
Where the wild things lead, we meet.

Nature's Sacred Wandering

Beneath the boughs where shadows blend,
We walk the trails that nature sends.
With every rustle, secrets hum,
In quietude, we find the drum.

The mountains rise, soliloquies,
In every breeze, a whispered tease.
The rivers dance, the pathways light,
In nature's fold, we take our flight.

With feet upon the mossy earth,
We witness all of nature's birth.
Each flower's bloom, a sacred rite,
In every shade, we find our light.

Through golden fields, we roam so free,
In harmony, a symphony.
The trees will guide, the winds advise,
In every breath, life's deep reprise.

A calling strong from deep within,
The pulse of life, we breathe akin.
In harmony, we hear the song,
Nature's sacred wandering, we belong.

With open hearts, we seek the truth,
In every moment, renew our youth.
A journey blessed by skies above,
In nature's arms, we find our love.

The Beauty of Unplanned Moments

Wander where the wildflowers grow,
In chaos, beauty starts to flow.
Unexpected paths we dare to tread,
Moments cherished, never led.

A gentle smile, a stranger's light,
In the unplanned, hearts take flight.
Fleeting seconds, memories bloom,
Joy erupts in every room.

Whispers of fate, a soft embrace,
In spontaneity, we find our place.
Life's surprise, a dance of chance,
With each turn, we learn to dance.

Laughter echoes through the air,
In every moment, love lays bare.
Untangled threads, a woven scheme,
Unplanned beauty, like a dream.

So let us roam, let spirit soar,
In every misstep, we explore.
The beauty lies in the unknown,
In unplanned moments, we have grown.

Grooves of the Traveler's Path

Wanderlust calls in a whispering breeze,
Footsteps finding rhythm with ease.
Every trail tells a story untold,
In the grooves, adventures unfold.

Mountains rise, and rivers flow,
Each mile traveled, we come to know.
The warmth of sun, the cool of night,
In nature's arms, everything feels right.

Through winding roads and dusty lanes,
Embracing joy, dismissing pains.
The traveler's heart beats wild and free,
In every twist, we find our glee.

The laughter shared on paths less worn,
In every footstep, a soul reborn.
With every sight, a memory made,
In the traveler's groove, life won't fade.

So wander on, with heart and soul,
Let the journey be your ultimate goal.
In every landscape that we traverse,
The world awaits; it's ours to disperse.

Embracing Change's Embrace

Life's river flows, ever anew,
Change spins tales, both old and true.
In every shift, we learn and grow,
A dance of seasons, ebb and flow.

Leaves turn gold, the air feels light,
Embracing change, our spirits ignite.
Through every trial, we find our grace,
In life's embrace, we find our place.

With courage, we walk through open doors,
Discovering dreams on distant shores.
The beauty found in each surprise,
In change, we find our skies.

So let us cherish every turn,
In the flame of growth, we brightly burn.
With open hearts, we face the dawn,
In change's arms, we are reborn.

Through every storm, we stand together,
In change, we find our strongest tether.
Embracing life, its ebb and flow,
In every change, our spirits grow.

A Symphony of Serendipity

Notes of chance weave through the air,
In serendipity, we find our care.
A whispered laugh, a gaze that meets,
In moments small, our heartbeats greet.

The world aligns in perfect rhyme,
Creating tunes beyond all time.
In unexpected turns, we find delight,
In serendipity, the stars ignite.

The magic found in every glance,
Like melodies, life leads us to dance.
A chance encounter, a guiding light,
In serendipity, we take flight.

With open hearts, we chase the song,
In every right, we embrace the wrong.
Each note and chord, a tale to weave,
In life's symphony, we believe.

So tune your heart to a joyous beat,
Let serendipity be your sweet.
In every echo, love takes a stand,
In this symphony, we are hand in hand.

In the Midst of Changing Scenery

Leaves flutter down, in hues of gold,
Whispers of autumn, stories untold.
Mountains stand tall, touched by the sun,
The canvas of nature, forever spun.

A river flows swiftly, reflecting the sky,
Mirroring dreams as they drift by.
Clouds drift like secrets, high above,
Casting their shadows, in silence and love.

Fields wave gently, in the soft breeze,
Nature's own dance, with perfect ease.
A bridge of memories, crossing time's span,
In every moment, the heart understands.

Birds take flight, tracing arcs of grace,
Chasing horizons, in a boundless space.
With each turn, life's colors blend,
In the midst of change, we find a friend.

As night falls softly, stars start to gleam,
Lighting the path of a whispered dream.
In the vast expanse of twilight's embrace,
We learn to find beauty in every place.

The Weight of a Thousand Journeys

Beneath the stars, footsteps softly tread,
Each one a tale, of where we've led.
Mountains climbed high, valleys traveled low,
In each shared memory, the heart's light glows.

Fleeting moments, treasures we hold,
The stories of love, of courage bold.
With every horizon, there's more to seek,
In the weight of journeys, the soul grows sleek.

Worn leather boots, and paths untraced,
Every step forward, an embrace of space.
The echoes of laughter, the tears we shed,
In the book of life, those moments are spread.

Maps may be tattered, but dreams still shine,
Navigating through chaos, we learn to align.
For every sorrow, a joy will emerge,
In the weight of journeys, we find our urge.

As time ticks on, we gather our threads,
Woven adventures, where destiny leads.
With hearts wide open, we journey on,
Carrying the weight, till dawn greets the dawn.

Threads of Whimsy and Wonder

In a world painted with light and hue,
Magic unfolds in everything we do.
Dancing butterflies, secrets at play,
Threads of whimsy, weave dreams of the day.

A sprinkle of laughter, a dash of delight,
In every small moment, joy takes flight.
Clouds like cotton, drifting in glee,
Where imagination flows, endlessly free.

The sun casts shadows, a playful design,
Crafting adventures, both yours and mine.
With each gentle breeze, whispers ignite,
Threads of wonder stitch day into night.

A child's bright smile, a story unfolds,
In little curiosities, life gently molds.
Every glance, a moment to treasure,
In the tapestry woven, we find our pleasure.

As starlight twinkles, dreams wish to explore,
Amidst the whimsy, we yearn for more.
With hearts as our compass, let's wander and see,
Threads of whimsy and wonder, sewn into our spree.

Piecing Together the Unknown

Fragments of thoughts, scattered like leaves,
Puzzle of life, where mystery weaves.
In shadows and light, the truth may unfold,
Piecing together stories yet untold.

Questions arise, like stars in the night,
Searching for answers, igniting the light.
Each twist and turn, a clue to embrace,
In the unknown's dance, we find our place.

With every step taken, the path becomes clear,
Trusting the journey, embracing the near.
The courage to question, the strength to seek,
In the unknown's wonder, our spirits speak.

Whispers of dreams, in echoes they bounce,
Gathering pieces, madly we pounce.
In life's great mosaic, we blend and align,
Creating a picture, where stars brightly shine.

As the tapestry forms, with colors so bright,
We embrace the chaos, we dance in the light.
In piecing together, the unknown we find,
The magic of living, the art of the mind.

Through the Forest of Time

In the stillness of the woods, it waits,
Leaves whisper secrets of worn-out fates.
Sunlight breaks through the ancient trees,
While shadows dance with the gentle breeze.

Footsteps echo on the forest floor,
Guiding souls to what they seek once more.
Paths of history intertwine and weave,
As time unfolds what we cannot perceive.

Birds sing tales that the wind has known,
In the heart of green, we are never alone.
Each rustling leaf tells of journeys past,
Through the forest's embrace, moments amass.

There's magic here beneath the boughs,
Every heartbeat, a quiet vow.
To cherish the silence, the stories that climb,
As we wander through the forest of time.

The Color of Experience

Shades of love paint the skies anew,
With every heartbeat, a vivid hue.
Joy splashes bright like the morning sun,
While sorrow's gray whispers we must shun.

Wisdom drapes itself in twilight's glow,
As lessons learned begin to flow.
Memories blend with strokes of regret,
Creating a canvas we won't forget.

Hope emerges as a gentle green,
In the garden of dreams silent and serene.
Each color a tale, each shade a fight,
The palette of life reflects our light.

With every brush, we interpret the past,
Through vibrant strokes, we find peace at last.
The color of experience hues our way,
Giving rise to a brand new day.

Echoes of Tomorrow

In the distance, whispers softly resound,
Echoes of dreams yet to be found.
Futures twinkle like stars in the night,
Guiding us gently toward the light.

Voices of hope mingle with the breeze,
Promises linger among the trees.
With every heartbeat, we forge a path,
Chasing shadows, evading the wrath.

Tomorrow's canvas awaits our strokes,
Filled with laughter and heartfelt jokes.
With courage as color, we paint it bright,
As echoes of yesterday fade from sight.

Dreams twist and turn in the dim twilight,
Transforming fears into pure delight.
Each echo a promise, a chance to fly,
In the embrace of the endless sky.

Beyond the Horizon's Edge

Where sky meets earth in whispered peace,
Waves of wonder begin to increase.
Beyond the horizon, new realms await,
With stories of solace from hands of fate.

Mountains rise high with secrets untold,
Challenging dreams, both timid and bold.
In the shadow of giants, we learn to stand,
Reaching for futures, we craft with our hands.

The sun dips low, painting skies aflame,
Every heartbeat whispers a name.
In the twilight glow, we find our way,
Beyond the horizon, there lies a day.

With each step forward, the world expands,
Boundless and bright in the open lands.
Beyond the horizon's edge, we will soar,
Embracing the journey forevermore.

Unfolding the Map Within

In quiet moments, we explore,
The treasures lying deep in store.
A heart that beats, a mind that dreams,
Awake the path with whispered gleams.

With every twist, with every turn,
We gather lessons, bright and stern.
Each winding road, a tale to tell,
In hidden corners, we know well.

The map unfolds, we start to see,
New lands of hope and mystery.
A journey rich with space to roam,
In every step, we find our home.

Through valleys low and mountains steep,
The spirit wakes, the soul will leap.
In shadows cast, in sunlight pure,
We find the strength to endure.

So take a breath, let go of fear,
Embrace the road that draws you near.
With every heartbeat, we're alive,
In this unfolding, we will thrive.

Stars Aligned on the Path

Night blankets the world in calm,
With cosmic whispers, like a psalm.
The stars above begin to shine,
A hint of fate, a thread divine.

As footsteps trace the silent ground,
In starlight's glow, our dreams abound.
The sky reflects our hopes so bright,
Guiding us through the dark of night.

Planets dance in rhythmic flow,
Their patterns guide the way we go.
Aligned above, we feel the call,
To trust the journey, give our all.

With constellations as our guide,
We learn to embrace the wild ride.
Each star a marker, strong and true,
In the celestial, we find clues.

So let your heart be gently swayed,
By every spark the night has laid.
The universe, in silence, speaks,
And in its light, our spirit seeks.

The Melody of Uncertainty

In echoes soft, an unknown tune,
Life plays along, beneath the moon.
Notes of doubt and sweet delight,
A dance that sways from day to night.

With every choice, the song expands,
A symphony in clumsy hands.
We seek the rhythm, only to find,
The sweetest sound is undefined.

The heartstrings pull, they twist and turn,
In every challenge, lessons burn.
Yet from the chaos, beauty grows,
In uncertain beats, our courage flows.

Let go of needing every note,
For freedom lives in the remote.
In dissonance, we find our grace,
In every stumble, life's embrace.

So hum along, though notes may stray,
In the uncertainty, find your way.
A melody that's yours to weave,
In every pause, believe, believe.

Conversations with the Wind

Whispers ride on zephyr's breath,
With secrets shared that tease of death.
The wind carries tales of the day,
In gentle swirls, it finds its way.

Rustling leaves, a soft embrace,
Speaking truths that time can't erase.
It beckons us to lean and hear,
The wisdom wrapped in silence near.

Through meadows wide and valleys deep,
The voice of nature, bold and steep.
In every gust, a story spins,
Of timelessness, where change begins.

So pause awhile, and feel its touch,
In laughter, sorrow — it holds so much.
A friend eternal, always near,
In conversations, we draw near.

With open hearts, let's learn to see,
The magic of the breeze set free.
For in the wind, we find a bond,
A promise whispered — we respond.

Emotes of the Open Road

With every mile, a dream unfolds,
The wind whispers secrets, stories untold.
Beneath the sky, a canvas of blue,
Adventure awaits in the morning dew.

Songs of freedom echo in my mind,
Each turn a new treasure, a path to find.
I chase the horizon, fearless and free,
The road is my guide, where I long to be.

Underneath stars that shimmer and glow,
I feel the pulse of the earth below.
Heartbeats in sync with the wheels on the ground,
In this vast expanse, true joy is found.

Through valleys and mountains, I wander and roam,
Each journey a chapter, each exit a home.
With laughter and joy, I savor the ride,
Emotes of the open road, my trusted guide.

As sunsets paint skies in hues of gold,
The memories linger, the tales unfold.
With every horizon that beckons anew,
The spirit of travel calls me to pursue.

The Spiral of Seeking

In the heart of the maze, I wander and muse,
With shadows as guides, I have nothing to lose.
Each question a circle, a path to behold,
The spiral of seeking reveals truths untold.

Footsteps lead deeper, where wisdom does flow,
In the silence between breaths, I learn to let go.
With every turn taken, a lesson unfolds,
In the spiral of seeking, the universe holds.

The mirrors of thought reflect back the light,
In the dance of the shadows, I discover what's right.
Whispers of yearning, of hope intertwined,
The spiral keeps turning, wisdom to find.

As I climb ever higher, the view starts to change,
Each layer revealing the beauty, the strange.
With courage, I navigate, embrace what I see,
In the spiral of seeking, I set my soul free.

Embrace all the questions, the doubts, and the fear,
For in each twist and turn, the answers draw near.
The journey is endless, yet filled with delight,
The spiral of seeking, my compass, my light.

Chasing Echoes of Yesterday

Faint whispers of laughter hang in the air,
Memories dance lightly, a soft, tender care.
I chase after echoes that drift on the breeze,
Finding warmth in the past, like sunlight through trees.

Each moment a fragment, a piece of my soul,
Collecting the echoes that make me feel whole.
Through corridors of time, I wander with grace,
Chasing the shadows, each familiar face.

The colors of autumn remind me of spring,
A tapestry woven, each thread a new fling.
In the laughter and tears, the lessons abide,
Chasing echoes of yesterday, my heart open wide.

With every glance backward, there's growth in the now,
A dance with the past, and I take my bow.
For in every moment, both fleeting and bright,
Chasing echoes of yesterday, I find my light.

The rhythm of time beats steady and true,
In echoes of yesterdays, I discover the new.
Embracing the journey, both old and the fresh,
Chasing echoes of yesterday, I find my flesh.

Navigating Through the Unfamiliar

Mist shrouds the landscape, a canvas of grey,
With wonder on my lips, I step into the fray.
Each path unwinds softly, a tale to unfold,
Navigating through the unfamiliar, brave and bold.

Whispers of the wild call out with a thrill,
Inviting me deeper, beyond every hill.
A heart full of courage, I venture inside,
In the maze of the new, my spirit takes pride.

With every heartbeat, there's magic in fear,
The unknown is calling, and the way feels clear.
Like stars in the night, I'm guided anew,
Navigating through the unfamiliar, dreams to pursue.

The strangers I meet share stories unchained,
In their eyes, I find wisdom, laughter ingrained.
Each moment a bridge to build with my heart,
Navigating through the unfamiliar, my new start.

As dawn breaks the silence, a promise awakes,
In every experience, the world gently shakes.
With open arms, I embrace every call,
Navigating through the unfamiliar, I'll rise, never fall.

The Embrace of New Beginnings

In the dawn's gentle light,
Hope whispers soft and clear,
Every day a fresh start,
Wiping away the fear.

With each step we take,
New dreams begin to bloom,
Filling the empty spaces,
With joy that overcomes the gloom.

Twisting paths unfold,
As the past fades away,
Embrace what lies ahead,
In the warmth of today.

A tender heart beats strong,
Guiding through the unknown,
Together we will rise,
In unity, we're grown.

Let the fresh winds blow,
Carrying scents of change,
In every breath we take,
Life's beauty rearranged.

Longing for the Open Sky

Underneath the wide expanse,
Wings whisper of the free,
Clouds drifting like our dreams,
Yearning for the sea.

Mountains call with voices strong,
Echoes in the breeze,
Heartbeats align with nature,
In a dance with trees.

The stars gaze down with wonder,
A canvas deep and bright,
Illuminating pathways,
In the calm of night.

Restless souls seek freedom,
Beyond the bounds we know,
Chasing hope and promise,
As the wild winds blow.

In every breath we take,
The sky's vastness calls,
We dream of open spaces,
And break down the walls.

Paths of Purpose and Wonder

Each step a story woven,
In the tapestry of time,
Purpose lights the shadows,
Infusing life with rhyme.

Curious hearts wander far,
Through valleys green and wide,
Finding joy in small things,
With love as their guide.

Underneath the starlit veil,
Wonders sit and wait,
Inviting us to follow,
To open every gate.

Mountains high and rivers deep,
Every challenge faced,
Building strength through struggle,
With memories embraced.

Within the paths we travel,
Every moment shines bright,
For purpose lends us courage,
And wonder guides our flight.

Along the Lines of Life

Life flows like a river,
With twists and turns that guide,
Moments weave together,
In the currents we abide.

Through laughter and through sorrow,
Each line a story spun,
We learn, we love, we wander,
Until the journey's done.

With every path we travel,
Lessons come to light,
In the dance of shadows,
We find our own true sight.

Hands held across the ages,
Bridges built from grace,
Together we find beauty,
In the sacred space.

Along the lines of life,
Connections intertwine,
A tapestry of moments,
In love, we brightly shine.

Milton Keynes UK
Ingram Content Group UK Ltd.
UKHW022118251124
451529UK00012B/590

9 789916 896204